SandCastle™

Primeros Sonidos

Raquel y Joaquín

Cathy Camarena, M.Ed., and Gloria B. Ruff, M.Ed.

Consulting Editors

Lourdes Flores-Hanson, M.S.E., and Gloria Rosso-White

ABDO Publishing Company

capstone®

www.capstoneclassroom.com

Credits
Curriculum Coordinator: Nancy Tuminelly
Cover and Interior Design and Production: Mighty Media
Child Photography: Steven Wewerka, Wewerka Photography
Photo Credits: AbleStock, Comstock, Eyewire Images, ShutterStock, Stockbyte

ISBN 978-1-4966-0365-4 (paperback)

Printed in the United States of America.
874

SandCastle™ books are created by a professional team of educators, reading specialists, and content developers around five essential components that include phonemic awareness, phonics, vocabulary, text comprehension, and fluency. All books are written, reviewed, and leveled for guided and early intervention reading, and designed for use in shared, guided, and independent reading and writing activities to support a balanced approach to literacy instruction.

SandCastle Level: Beginning

Qq

ABCChDEFGH
IJKLLLMNÑOP
QRSTUVWXYZ

abcchdefgh
ijklllmnñop
qrstuvwxyz

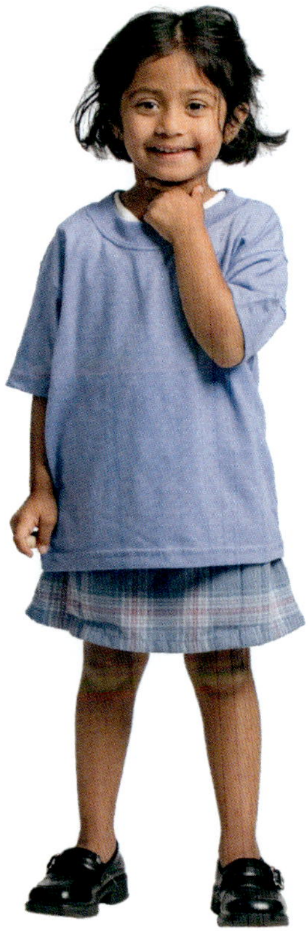

Raquel

Joaquín

panqueque

queso

mariquita

querubín

15

quince

El  está aquí.

El  está aquí.

La  está aquí.

Aquí está el .

Mira el número 15.

A Raquel y a Joaquín le gustan los panqueques.

Los panqueques son grandes.

Los panqueques están sabrosos.

Raquel y Joaquín comen quince panqueques.

¿Cuáles de estas cosas contienen **que/qui**?

15

Más palabras que contienen que/qui

chaqueta

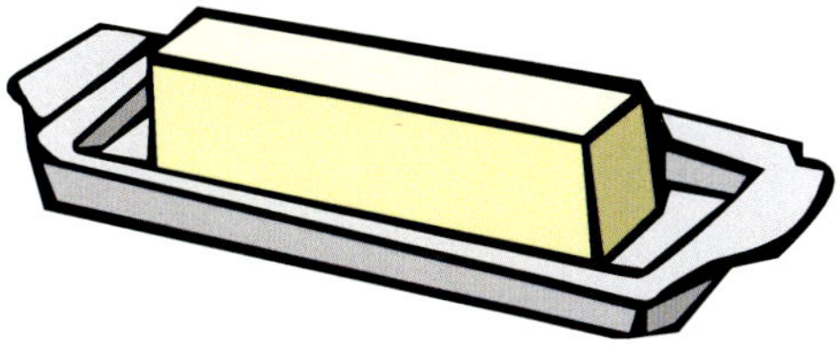

mantequilla

quesadilla

500

quinientos

quiosco

About SandCastle™

A professional team of educators, reading specialists, and content developers created the SandCastle™ series to support young readers as they develop reading skills and strategies and increase their general knowledge. The SandCastle™ series has four levels that correspond to early literacy development in young children. The levels are provided to help teachers and parents select the appropriate books for young readers.

Emerging Readers
(no flags)

Beginning Readers
(1 flag)

Transitional Readers
(2 flags)

Fluent Readers
(3 flags)

These levels are meant only as a guide. All levels are subject to change.

ABDO Publishing Company
www.abdopub.com

capstone®
www.capstoneclassroom.com